W9-BQV-225

★ ★

HAWAII

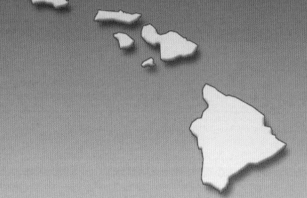

by William David Thomas

GARETH**STEVENS**

GS

P U B L I S H I N G

Please visit our web site at: www.garethstevens.com
For a free color catalog describing Gareth Stevens Publishing's
list of high-quality books and multimedia programs, call
1-800-542-2595 (USA) or 1-800-387-3178 (Canada).
Gareth Stevens Publishing's fax: (414) 332-3567.

Library of Congress Cataloging-in-Publication Data

Thomas, William, 1947-
    Hawaii / William David Thomas.
      p. cm. — (Portraits of the states)
    Includes bibliographical references and index.
    ISBN-10: 0-8368-4699-0 — ISBN-13: 978-0-8368-4699-7 (lib. bdg.)
    ISBN-10: 0-8368-4716-4 — ISBN-13: 978-0-8368-4716-1 (softcover)
    1. Hawaii—Juvenile literature. I. Title. II. Series.
    DU623.25.T56   2007
    996.9—dc22   2006001900

This edition first published in 2007 by
Gareth Stevens Publishing
A Member of the WRC Media Family of Companies
330 West Olive Street, Suite 100
Milwaukee, WI 53212 USA

This edition copyright © 2007 by Gareth Stevens, Inc.

Editorial direction: Mark J. Sachner
Project manager: Jonatha A. Brown
Editor: Catherine Gardner
Art direction and design: Tammy West
Picture research: Diane Laska-Swanke
Indexer: Walter Kronenberg
Production: Jessica Morris and Robert Kraus

Picture credits: Cover, © Tom Bean; pp. 4, 18, 20, 21, 22, 24, 27 © John Elk III;
p. 5 © Brandon Cole/Visuals Unlimited; p. 6 © North Wind Picture Archives;
p. 8 © Bettmann/CORBIS; pp. 9, 16 © CORBIS; p. 11 © Hulton Archive/Getty
Images; p. 12 © Leonard McCombe/Time & Life Pictures/Getty Images; p. 15
© Gibson Stock Photography; pp. 25, 28, 29 © AP Images; p. 26 © Jeff
Greenberg/PhotoEdit

Printed in the United States of America

1 2 3 4 5 6 7 8 9 10 09 08 07 06

CONTENTS

Words that are defined in the Glossary appear
in **bold** the first time they are used in the text.

On the Cover: Hawaii has lots of warm blue water, sun, sand, and palm
trees. This beautiful beach is on the island of Kauai.

Introduction

Aloha! One meaning of this Hawaiian word is "welcome!"

Hawaii welcomes millions of visitors every year. They come from all over the world. They swim in the warm blue water. They relax on white sandy beaches. Some climb volcanoes, play golf, or watch whales.

This state is different from most of the other U.S. states. It is not just one piece of land. It is made up of many islands. One of them is named Hawaii, but the whole state is named Hawaii, too.

The people who live in Hawaii came from many places. The differences in their manners, speech, and food make the state even more interesting.

Visit the warm, sunny islands of Hawaii. Welcome! Aloha!

Poipu Beach is on the island of Kauai. Beautiful places like this bring millions of visitors to Hawaii each year.

The state flag of Hawaii.

HAWAII FACTS

- Became the 50th U.S. State: August 21, 1959
- Population (2004): 1,262,840
- Capital: Honolulu
- Biggest Cities: Honolulu, Hilo, Kailua, Kaneohe
- Size: 6,423 square miles (16,636 square kilometers)
- Nickname: The Aloha State
- State Bird: Nene (Hawaiian goose)
- State Marine Mammal: Humpback whale
- State Flower: Pua aloalo (yellow hibiscus)
- State Tree: Kukui (candlenut)

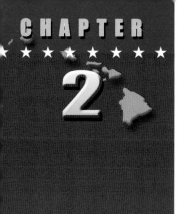
History

Far off in the South Pacific Ocean is a group of small islands. They are called the Marquesas. About seventeen hundred years ago, some men and women decided to leave these islands. They filled their big canoes with seeds, food, and some small animals. They paddled and sailed across the ocean for many days. At last, they saw land. The land they saw is now called Hawaii.

These people settled on this land. They built houses near the ocean. They planted gardens and fished in the sea.

The First Europeans and the First King

James Cook was an English sea captain. He came to Hawaii in 1778. He probably was the first European to see these islands. Cook named them the Sandwich Islands.

Soon after Cook's visit, a great chief took control of the island of Hawaii. He

The first Native Hawaiians built their homes near the ocean. They used canoes for fishing and to travel among the islands.

fought battles with the chiefs on the other islands. At last, this great chief became the king. King Kamehameha (ka-MAY-ha-MAY-ha) I was the first person to rule all of the islands of Hawaii.

Americans Arrive

By 1819, ships from the United States were coming to Hawaii. The sailors were hunting for whales. Stores were built to sell goods to the sailors. Towns began to grow. Some **ports** became very busy. One of the ports was Honolulu, on the island of Oahu.

A group of **missionaries** arrived in 1820. They came from Boston, Massachusetts. They wanted the Hawaiians to become Christians. The missionaries built churches and started the first schools in Hawaii. They learned the

The Earl of Sandwich

John Montagu was an English nobleman. He was the Earl of Sandwich. He helped pay for Captain Cook's ship and sailors. When Cook reached the Hawaiian Islands, he named them for the Earl. Montagu was a very busy man. An old story says he did not like to stop to eat. At mealtime, he ate meat between two pieces of bread. People began calling these quick meals "a sandwich."

Hawaiian language and wrote it down. That was the first time Hawaiian was written. One of the first books that was **translated** into Hawaiian was the Bible.

The sailors, missionaries, and white settlers brought new diseases to the islands.

FACTS

Surf's Up!

Captain Cook's sailors saw Hawaiian men riding ocean waves on wooden boards. They were surfing! The Hawaiians called it *he'e nalu*. That means "wave sliding." Surfing is still very popular in Hawaii.

During the 1800s, thousands of people came to Hawaii from China and Japan. They worked in the sugar cane fields. These people brought their languages and beliefs with them.

Many Native Hawaiians became sick and died.

Sugar Brings Changes

The missionaries and their families began buying lots of land. They started big farms called **plantations**. They planted sugar cane. It was used to make sugar. The sugar was sold in the United States. It was called "Sandwich Island sugar." It became very popular. That brought lots of money to the plantation owners.

Soon, more workers were needed. The plantation owners brought people from other lands. Starting in 1852, thousands of workers came to the islands. At first, they came from China. Later, workers came from Japan.

The workers from China and Japan brought their languages and customs. Their ways started to mix with the languages and customs of the whites and Native people. In time, the **culture** of the islands began to change.

New Territory

The plantation owners soon controlled all of the banks. They controlled the ships that brought goods to and from Hawaii. They also made many of the laws for the islands.

In 1891, Liliuokalani (LEE-lee-oo-oh-ka-LAN-ee) became the first queen of Hawaii. She did not want the islands run by white

IN HAWAII'S HISTORY

Stealing the Islands

Sanford Dole was the son of missionaries. He became a lawyer, and then, a judge. He helped the sugar growers in Hawaii get more land and power. Dole helped force Queen Liliuokalani to give up the throne in 1893. This action took power away from native Hawaiians. The next year, Dole became president of Hawaii. When the islands became a U.S. **territory**, Dole was named the governor. One hundred years later, U.S. President Bill Clinton said that what Dole and the others did was wrong. Clinton apologized to the Hawaiian people.

Sanford B. Dole helped plantation owners take control of the islands away from native Hawaiians.

9

Famous People of Hawaii

Father Damien (Joseph De Veuster)

Born: January 3, 1840, Tremelo, Belgium

Died: April 15, 1889, Kalaupapa, Molokai, Hawaii

Father Damien was a Roman Catholic priest. He came to Hawaii in 1865. He learned about Hawaiians who had **leprosy**. It was a terrible disease. People who had this disease were forced to live far away from other people. In Hawaii, they lived on the island of Molokai. Father Damien moved there. He did all he could for the sick people. Finally, he caught leprosy himself. Father Damien died on Molokai in 1889. A home for people with this disease is still there.

businessmen. She wanted Native Hawaiians to control the islands.

Plantation owners became angry and worried. In 1893, some of them went to the queen's palace, along with U.S. soldiers. They forced her to give up power. They took over the government. That was the end of kings and queens in Hawaii. In 1900, Hawaii became a U.S. territory.

At about this same time, some plantation owners began to grow pineapples. In 1992, a white man named James Dole bought the island of Lanai. He made a pineapple plantation on this island. The pineapple became big business in Hawaii.

World War II

After Hawaii became a territory, the U.S. Navy began keeping ships in a port near Honolulu. It was called Pearl Harbor.

By 1941, thousands of soldiers and sailors lived at Pearl Harbor. It was the most important U.S. **military** base in the Pacific Ocean.

The USS Arizona burned and sank when the Japanese attacked Pearl Harbor. More than 1,100 men died on the ship.

IN HAWAII'S HISTORY

A Royal Song

After Queen Liliuokalani was forced from power, she began to write. She wrote poetry and songs. One day, she watched two sweethearts saying goodbye. She wrote a song about it called "Aloha Oe." That means "farewell to you." Today, her song is famous.

On December 7, 1941, Japanese warplanes bombed Pearl Harbor. More than twenty-three hundred people died. Many airplanes and ships were destroyed. The United States went to war with Japan the next day. World War II lasted almost four more years.

Statehood

After the war, many Hawaiians wanted to make

11

When Hawaii became a state in 1959, people celebrated with drummng, singing, and dancing. The American flag was changed from forty-nine stars to fifty. The fiftieth star was for Hawaii.

IN HAWAII'S HISTORY

Asian American Firsts

The people of Hawaii are proud to claim two important "firsts" in U.S. history. Hiram Fong's parents came to Hawaii from China. In 1959, Fong became the state's first U.S. senator. He also was the first Asian American to be elected to the Senate. He served for eighteen years. George Ariyoshi's family came from Japan. In 1974, Ariyoshi became the first Japanese American to be elected governor of a U.S. state. He was Hawaii's governor for thirteen years.

the islands a state. Some people were against the idea. They were unhappy about the large number of Japanese people living in Hawaii. An election was held to decide. Ninety percent of the people voted for statehood. Hawaii became the fiftieth state on August 21, 1959.

Soon after that, a new business began to grow. It was **tourism**. Airplanes and faster ships made it easier for people to travel to the islands. Hotels opened up near many of the beaches. Tourism soon became more important than the sugar and pineapple crops. Today, Hawaii is one of the world's most popular vacation spots.

★ ★ ★ Time Line ★ ★ ★

300	People from the Marquesas Islands reach Hawaii.
1778–1779	Captain James Cook visits the islands.
1810	King Kamehameha I becomes the first king to rule all of Hawaii.
1819	Whaling ships come to the islands.
1820	Missionaries from the United States arrive in Hawaii.
1852	People from China begin coming to Hawaii to work on sugar plantations.
1868	Japanese plantation workers arrive in Hawaii.
1893	Queen Liliuokalani is overthrown by white businessmen.
1900	Hawaii becomes a U.S. territory.
1941	Japan attacks Pearl Harbor, bringing the United States into World War II.
1959	Hawaii becomes the fiftieth U.S. state.
1986	Hawaiian astronaut Ellison Onizuka dies on the space shuttle *Challenger*.
1993	President Clinton apologizes to Hawaiians for taking their land.
2005	Hawaiian teenager Michelle Wie becomes a professional golfer.

People

Almost three-fourths of all the people in Hawaii live on the island of Oahu. Most of them live in or near Honolulu. This city is a center for business, travel, and government. The state's other islands have far fewer people. Hilo, on the island of Hawaii, is the second-largest city. It is much smaller than Honolulu.

Today, Hawaii's islands are home to a great mix of people. Some of the people in the state are Native Hawaiian. They work hard to keep their culture alive.

Hispanics

This chart shows the different racial backgrounds of people in Hawaii. In the 2000 U.S. Census, 7.2 percent of the people in Hawaii called themselves Latino or Hispanic. Most of them or their relatives came from places where Spanish is spoken. Hispanics do not appear on this chart because they may come from any racial background.

The People of Hawaii

Total Population 1,262,840

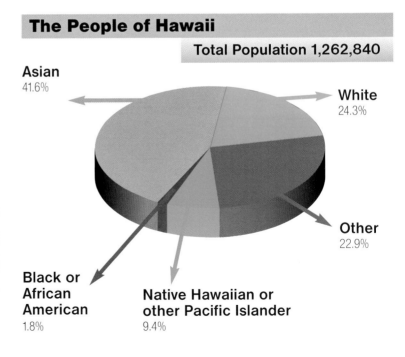

Asian 41.6%

White 24.3%

Other 22.9%

Black or African American 1.8%

Native Hawaiian or other Pacific Islander 9.4%

Percentages are based on the 2000 Census.

Language

The Hawaiian language is one official language in the state. English is the other. The Hawaiian alphabet is one of the shortest in the world. In all, it has only twelve letters. The five vowels are *a, e, i, o,* and *u.* The seven other letters are *h, k, l, m, n, p,* and *w.* Here are some Hawaiian words.

Ae (AH-ay) means "yes."

Aole (ah-OH-lay) is the word for "no."

Mahalo (ma-HA-lo) is the word for "thank you."

Aloha (ah-LO-ha) means "welcome." It also can mean "goodbye." It can even mean "love to you."

Hawaii also has a third language, called Pidgin. It is a mix of English, Hawaiian, and some Asian languages.

These girls are learning to dance the hula. Classes like this help keep Native island culture alive.

Many people in the islands speak Pidgin. Someone might say, *"Da kine grinds Hawaii mo bettah."* That means, "The food in Hawaii is really good."

Many Cultures

In the rest of the United States, most people are white. In Hawaii, Asians are the largest group. Many of them, or their relatives, came from China and Japan. People came from Korea and the Philippines, too. These people are Americans now, but they want to keep their old culture as well. They celebrate the holidays of their homeland and hold festivals. Some teach their language to their children and others.

Honolulu is Hawaii's capital and its biggest city. More than 370,000 people live here. Notice the beaches close to the city.

FACTS

The Hula

Hawaiians have danced the hula for hundreds of years. At first, drums and voices were the only music. Hula songs and movements were religious. They also told stories and history. The missionaries did not like hula and tried to stop it. Today, special schools teach hula. The music often comes from guitars and **ukuleles**, instead of drums.

Religion

Early Hawaiians worshipped many gods. They built stone temples for these gods. The old religion died out after the missionaries came. The first ones were Protestants. Catholics and others soon followed them. Today, many Christian faiths have built churches in Hawaii. People who came from China and Japan brought Buddhism to Hawaii. The state also has a small Jewish population.

Education

King Kamehameha III started Hawaii's first public school system. That was in 1840. Much has changed since then. Today, all public schools are run by the State Board of Education. It runs all of the public libraries in Hawaii, too.

After high school, many students go to the University of Hawaii. Its ten **campuses** are in towns and cities on four different islands. About forty-five thousand students go there each year.

Famous People of Hawaii

Duke Kahanamoku

Born: August 24, 1890, Honolulu, Oahu, Hawaii

Died: January 22, 1968, Honolulu, Oahu, Hawaii

Duke Kahanamoku was a Native Hawaiian and a great swimmer. He swam in the Olympic Games three times and won five medals. In 1984, he was voted into the Olympic Hall of Fame. Duke also liked surfing. He started one of the first surfing clubs on Waikiki Beach. Duke made surfing popular in California and Australia, too.

The Land

The state of Hawaii has more than 130 islands. They are in the Pacific Ocean, far from the rest of the United States. The eight main islands were made by volcanoes.

Kauai

Kauai is called "the Garden Island." It has rugged mountains and rain forests. Mt. Waialeale gets more rain than almost any other place on Earth. The Waimea River has cut a deep canyon on the island. It brings many hikers to Kauai.

Oahu

Oahu has more people and is more crowded than the other islands. The state capital, Honolulu, is on this island. Oahu

---

FUN FACTS

Madam Pele

Long ago in Hawaii, people believed Pele (PAY-lay) was the goddess of fire. Today, some Hawaiians say that Pele lives inside the volcano called Kilauea. When she becomes angry, the volcano may erupt. They try to keep Pele happy. People do not take stones from this volcano. Some leave gifts for this fiery spirit.

Hikers love Waimea Canyon on the island of Kauai. Waimea Canyon is known as "the Grand Canyon of the Pacific."

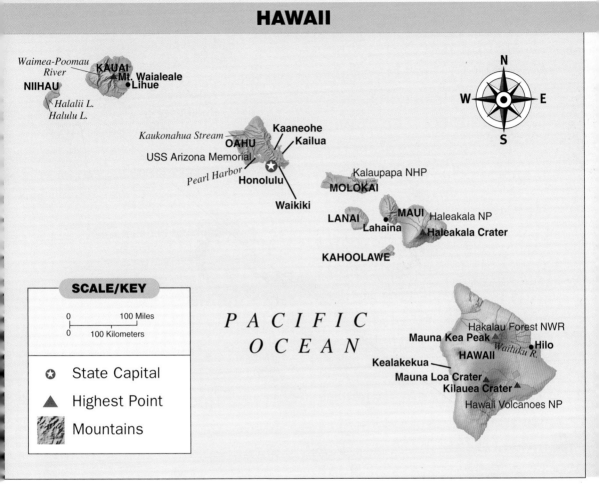

has many beaches. One of the most famous is Waikiki Beach. Not far from there is Diamond Head. Once, this famous hill was a volcano.

Molokai

Molokai is the most **rural** of the five biggest islands. It has sheep and cattle ranches.

The world's tallest sea cliffs are on the north side of the island. These cliffs go nearly straight up from the ocean. Some of them are 3,300 feet (1,006 meters) high.

Maui

Maui is the second-largest island. It has sandy beaches

all around its coast. One famous place is Haleakala. This is a volcano that no longer erupts. The **crater** of this dead volcano is the largest in the world.

Hawaii

Hawaii is the largest island. It is called "the Big Island." This island has two active volcanoes. One of them is Kilauea. This volcano has been erupting since 1983. Another volcano, called Mauna Kea, is the tallest mountain in the state. It is 13,796 feet (4,205 m) high. The state's second-largest city, called Hilo, is on the island of Hawaii.

Smaller Islands

No one lives on Kahoolawe. The

This is the crater of Haleakala, a dead volcano on Maui.

Major Rivers

Kaukonahua Stream (South Fork)
33 miles (53 km) long

Wailuku River
32 miles (51 km) long

Waimea-Poomau River
20 miles (32 km) long

U.S. military once used this island as a bombing target. The island of Lanai was a pineapple plantation at one time. Now, it is being made into a resort. Niihau is the smallest of the main islands. It is known as the Forbidden Island. People own Niihau. No one can go there except their guests.

This large bird is a nene, or Hawaiian goose. It is the State Bird. Some birds in Hawaii are found nowhere else on Earth.

Ride 'Em, Paniolo!
Cowboys in Hawaii? You bet! The Parker Ranch is on the Big Island. It is one of the largest cattle ranches in the United States. The cowboys on the ranch are called *paniolos*. On the Fourth of July, the Parker Ranch has horse races and a rodeo.

Plants and Animals

Hawaii is famous for its tropical flowers. Hibiscus blossoms come in many colors. Hawaiian orchids are sent all over the world.

Some of Hawaii's birds are very rare. They cannot be found anywhere else on Earth. Many of them are now **endangered**. People in the state are trying to protect these birds. Otherwise, they may disappear forever.

Hawaii has few wild land animals, but it has many sea animals. The ocean around Hawaii is home to hundreds of kinds of fish. Whales, dolphins, seals, sharks, and turtles swim there too.

A Sunny Spot

Hawaii is warm all year. Some parts of the state get lots of rain. Other parts are dry. Most places, however, get lots of sunshine.

21

Economy

Sugar and pineapple were Hawaii's most important products for many years. Now, they are not as important as they once were. The United States buys most of its sugar and pineapple from other countries.

The Military

The U.S. government owns lots of land in Hawaii. It has more than one hundred military sites just on the island of Oahu. More soldiers and sailors live in Hawaii than in any other state. Many have their families with them.

Millions of visitors come to Hawaii each year for the sun and water. Tourism is the state's biggest business.

Tourism

The biggest business in the state is tourism. Millions of visitors come here every year. Most of them come to Oahu, Hawaii, and Maui.

Tourists make jobs for lots of people. Workers in stores that sell swimsuits, flowers, and film are all part of the tourist business. Many lifeguards, singers, dancers, and taxi drivers have jobs in places where tourists visit. Hotel and restaurant workers are in the tourist business, too.

People who have jobs that help other people are called service workers. Many of Hawaii's service workers help tourists. Some of the other service workers in the state are teachers, doctors, and nurses.

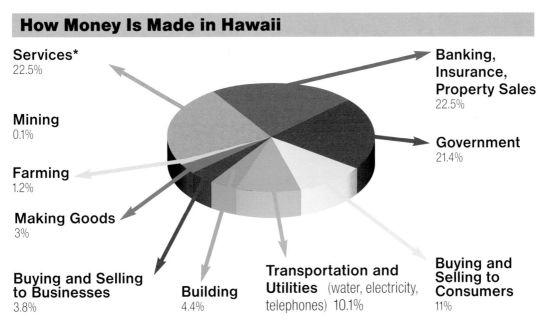

How Money Is Made in Hawaii

Services*
22.5%

Mining
0.1%

Farming
1.2%

Making Goods
3%

Banking,
Insurance,
Property Sales
22.5%

Government
21.4%

Buying and Selling
to Businesses
3.8%

Building
4.4%

Transportation and
Utilities (water, electricity,
telephones) 10.1%

Buying and
Selling to
Consumers
11%

* Services include jobs in hotels, restaurants, auto repair, medicine, teaching, and entertainment.

Government

Hawaii's state government is like the government of the United States. It has three parts, called branches. These parts are the executive, legislative, and judicial branches.

Executive Branch

The executive branch carries out the laws of the state. It is led by the governor. The lieutenant governor helps the governor. Many other officials also work in this branch.

Hawaii's state capitol building is in Honolulu.

Legislative Branch

The legislative branch makes the laws for the state. This branch has two parts. They are the Senate and the House of Representatives.

Judicial Branch

Courts and judges make up the judicial branch. They may decide whether a person who is accused of committing a crime is guilty.

Local Government

Hawaii has no city or town governments. Instead, the whole state is divided into four counties. Each county has a mayor and a council. These councils decide how land will be used. They also are in charge of fire and police services.

This is the Hawaii state Senate at work. Some of the lawmakers wear flower necklaces called leis. Many law makers wear brightly colored shirts instead of suits and ties.

HAWAII'S STATE GOVERNMENT

Executive		Legislative		Judicial	
Office	**Length of Term**	**Body**	**Length of Term**	**Court**	**Length of Term**
Governor	4 years	Senate (25 members)	4 years	Supreme (5 justices)	10 years
Lieutenant Governor	4 years	House of Representatives (51 members)	2 years	Intermediate Court of Appeals (6 judges)	10 years

Things to See and Do

Hawaii offers so many different things to see and do. There is something for everyone to enjoy in the Aloha State.

Love That Luau

Lots of people who visit Hawaii go to a luau (LOO-au). This is a big Hawaiian feast. You eat roast pig, fish, pineapple, and bananas. Most luaus have singing and dancing, too. A luau is a fun way to learn about Hawaiian culture.

FUN FACTS

Poi

At a luau, you may eat poi. This food has been made and eaten in Hawaii for hundreds of years. It is made from a plant called taro. The root of the taro is peeled, cut up, and boiled. Then, it is mashed into a thick, gooey paste. The **traditional** way to eat it is with your fingers!

At the Polynesian Cultural Center, you can enjoy singing and dancing and meet people from seven Pacific island groups.

You can learn even more at the Polynesian Cultural Center. It is near Honolulu. The people who work here come from seven different Pacific island groups. One of them is Hawaii. You can hear the language and music of these islands. You can see their dancing and try their food, too.

History and Festivals

You can learn about Hawaii's history in Honolulu at the Bishop Museum. One of

This memorial is at Pearl Harbor, near Honolulu. It rests above the battleship USS *Arizona*. The ship sank during the Japanese attack on December 7th, 1941.

Ellison Onizuka

Born: June 24, 1948, Kealakekua, Island of Hawaii, Hawaii

Died: January 28, 1986, Cape Canaveral, Florida

Ellison Onizuka was an officer in the U.S. Air Force. He trained to be an astronaut. In January 1985, he flew into space on the shuttle *Discovery*. He became the first Hawaiian and the first Japanese American in space. One year later, he died. He and six other crew members were killed when the space shuttle *Challenger* blew up soon after takeoff. Onizuka is remembered in Hawaii as a hero.

many things on display is a cloak made of feathers. It was once worn by King Kamehameha I. On Maui, you can visit a whaling museum in Lahaina. Or you can take a boat ride to see real whales!

Do you like flowers? The Nani Mau Gardens in Hilo are famous for their tropical blossoms. While you are on the Big Island, be sure to go to Volcanoes National Park. You may see hot lava flow into the ocean!

Each year Hawaii has Aloha Festivals that last for two months! These festivals take place all over the state. They have hula and singing contests, parades, and other celebrations. There are even bed races! In these races, teams of people push beds on wheels.

Madam Pele is angry! Here, lava from the Kilauea volcano on Hawaii flows into the Pacific Ocean. The lava cools and turns into rock. The volcano is actually making the Big Island bigger.

Famous People of Hawaii

Michelle Wie

Born: October 11, 1989, Honolulu, Oahu, Hawaii

In some ways, Michelle Wie is like most teens. She likes to hang out with friends. She likes computers. In other ways, Wie is very different. She is over 6 feet (1.8 m) tall. And she can really hit a golf ball. She began playing golf when she was four years old. She has played against some of the best women golfers in the world. When she was fourteen, she played in a golf **tournament** for men. Wie beat some of them. Just after her sixteenth birthday, she became a professional golfer.

Some of the world's best surfers come to Hawaii to ride the waves. At Waimea Beach, on the North Shore of Oahu, the waves may be twenty-five feet high. It is exciting, but dangerous!

Sports

Professional football comes to Hawaii in February. The best players in the National Football League play in the Pro Bowl in Honolulu.

Many people come to the islands to play golf all year long. Water sports are very popular, too. Surfing is an exciting sport to watch or do. You can paddle an ocean-going canoe or kayak. You can go fishing or swim in the ocean or a pool.

★ ★

campuses — the buildings and land that belong to a university

crater — the low, bowl-shaped space at the top of a volcano

culture — the language, dress, and customs of a group of people

endangered — at risk of becoming extinct

leprosy — a disease that causes skin and muscles to waste away

military — having to do with the armed forces

missionaries — people who go to another land to teach their religion

plantations — very large farms where the work is done by people who live there

ports — cities with harbors where ships can dock and load or unload goods or passengers

rural — in the country; far away from big cities and large towns

territory — an area that belongs to a country

tourism — encouraging visitors to come to a place

tournament — a sports contest for lots of teams or people

traditional — an old, honored way of doing things

translated — changed from one language to another

ukuleles — small guitars, with four strings, often used in Hawaiian music

Books

From the Mountains to the Sea: Early Hawaiian Life.
   Julie Stewart Williams (Kamehameha Schools Press)

Hawaii. Land of Liberty (series). Jody Sullivan
   (Capstone Press)

Hawaii Volcanoes National Park. Symbols of Freedom (series).
   Margaret C. Hall (Heinemann)

Last Princess: The Story of Princess Ka' iulani of Hawaii.
   Fay Stanley (HarperCollins)

Unique Animals of Hawaii. Regional Wild America (series).
   Lee Jacobs (Blackbirch Press)

Web Sites

A to Z Kid's Stuff: Hawaii
www.atozkidstuff.com/hawaii.html

Enchanted Learning: Hawaii
www.enchantedlearning.com/usa/states/hawaii/

Hawaii Kids
www.hawaiikids.net/kids/

Hawaii School Reports
www.hawaiischoolreports.com/culture/kids.htm

INDEX

12/06